KINO

His Missions, His Monuments

By

Charles W. Polzer, S.J.

Jesuit Fathers of Southern Arizona

Tucson   Arizona

1998

About This Book

KINO: His Missions, His Monuments is intended as a small guide to the "Kino" missions of northern Sonora and Southern Arizona. Published here as a separate book, it is a "break-out" from the larger and more comprehensive *KINO: A Legacy*. Both books evolved from the long selling *Kino Guide II* that remained as the classic mission guide for the region for more than two decades.

Knowing that the general public would want a less expensive yet relatively complete guide to the missions, this book is being sold under a separate title and cover. But in no way can it substitute for the compelling story of Padre Eusebio Francisco Kino, the Jesuit missionary explorer, who literally put these many towns and villages on the map. This small volume also contains the celebratory aspects of Kino's fame – the discovery of his grave, the construction of the memorial plaza, and the sculpting of several commemorative statues.

About the Author

Charles W. Polzer, S.J. is the curator of Ethnohistory at the Arizona State Museum and the resident head of the American Division of the Jesuit Historical Institute also at the Museum. He is a recognized Spanish colonial historian, and for some thirty years has engaged in the study of the Jesuit missions of northern New Spain.

About the Maps and Covers

The maps for this volume were drawn by Ray Harden of Tucson. His artistic talents were also responsible for the creation of the front covers for *KINO: A Legacy* and for *KINO: His Missions, His Monuments*. The back cover of each book comes through the courtesy of the DeGrazia Foundation; the reproduction is Ted DeGrazia's portrait of Kino on horseback from his collection of paintings on Padre Kino.

Library of Congress Catalog Card Number
LC97-92848

ISBN 0-9661562-1-8

CONTENTS

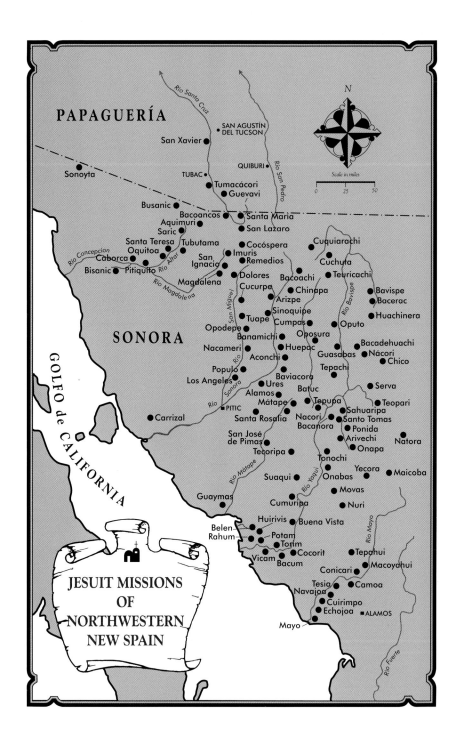

PAPAGUERÍA

SAN AGUSTÍN
DEL TUCSON

San Xavier

Sonoyta

QUIBURI

TUBAC

Tumacácori
Guevavi

Busanic

Bacoancos · Santa María
Aquimuri · San Lázaro
Saric

Santa Teresa Tubutama · Cocóspera · Cuquiarachi
Oquitoa · Imuris
Caborca · San · Remedios · Cuchuta
Ignacio
Bisanic · Pitiquito · Dolores · Bacoachi · Teuricachi
Magdalena · Cucurpe · Chinapa · Bavispe
Arizpe · Bacerac
Sinoquipe · Cumpas · Huachinera
SONORA · Tuape · Oputo
Opodepe · Banamichi · Oposura
Nacameri · Huepac · Bacadehuachi
Aconchi · Guasabas · Nácori
Populo · Tepachi · Chico
Los Angeles · Baviacora
Ures · Batuc · Serva
Alamos · Tepupa · Teopari
Mátape · Sahuaripa
Carrizal · Santa Rosalía · Nacori · Santo Tomas
Bacanora · Ponida
San José · Arivechi · Natora
de Pimas · Onapa
Tecoripa · Tonochi
Yecora · Maicoba
Suaqui · Onabas
Guaymas · Movas
Cumuripa · Nuri
Huirivis · Buena Vista
Belen
Rahum · Potam
Torim
Vicam · Bacum · Cocorit · Tepahui
Conicari · Macoyahui
Tesia · Camoa
Navajoa
Cuirimpo
Echojoa · ALAMOS
Mayo

GOLFO de CALIFORNIA

PITIC

N

Scale in miles

0   25   50

Rio Santa Cruz
Rio San Pedro
Rio Concepcion
Rio Altar
Rio Magdalena
San Miguel
Rio Sonora
Rio
Rio Mátape
Rio Yaqui
Rio Bavispe
Rio Mayo
Rio Fuerte

JESUIT MISSIONS
OF
NORTHWESTERN
NEW SPAIN

iv

THE MISSIONS OF PADRE KINO

Contemporary Americans seldom question their stereotypical concept of the "Spanish mission." Some concepts are pious ones – of devoted religious, obedient neophytes, and quaint churches in the wilderness. Some are impious – of domineering clerics, enslaved natives, and fortress compounds. How does the historian disabuse anyone of these commonly held ideas that have sprouted in the darkness of ignorance? One important task of history is to enlighten the past so that present and future generations can know the genuine contributions our predecessors have made.

Although we speak of the "Spanish mission" or the "mission system," in reality each mission recorded a distinct, even diverse, history. The net-works of missions in different regions and in different epochs may have been analogous, but they were certainly not the same. In northern New Spain (Mexico) five or six systems can be described, although they each conformed to the *Laws of the Indies*. The "Kino mission chain" in the Pimería Alta was only a segment of one of these systems.

The first two, and earliest, systems were formed along the spine of the Sierra Madre Occidental. In the late 16th century Franciscan Friars opened mission centers among the Chichimec tribes while the Jesuit Blackrobes labored along the Pacific slope. Franciscan evangelization in the central plateau occasioned their entry into New Mexico where the Spaniards encountered the highly organized Pueblo societies. By contrast the Jesuit missionaries more commonly dealt with scattered nations in the rugged mountains and river valleys of western Mexico. In the late 17th century the Jesuits opened a new chain of missions in Baja California that required significantly innovative procedures for administration and supply. At the same time the Franciscans pressed eastward into Texas where their missions played a dual role in conversion and frontier defense. When the missions of Alta California were established in the late 18th century, the role of the mission had undergone substantial modification due to the secular goals of military security and overland supply. Nowhere at any time was there a uniform mission system.

Unfortunately too many writers have created romantic fictions about mission life. As the story typically goes, a stalwart, rugged man of God rides into the wilderness and with bare hands builds a monumental church on an idyllic hilltop. Curious natives respond to reverberating bells; songs fill the air; and fields of grain wave in the golden sun. The splendor and abundance are irresistible. The truth, however, was quite different. Usually the new missionary rode into long established native villages under military escort; negotiations ensued in which the Indians decided to accept or decline the invitation to have a European living and working among them. Only after long years of patient ministry was a missionary able to penetrate new frontiers and find new peoples who might be eager to accept him and the Faith. It was almost exclusively a matter of the missionary's established reputation.

Missions were also successful to the extent that the initial enticements of food, clothing, and supplies led to the richer benefits of education and incorporation into the comparative opulence of Spanish society. Indeed, the Spaniard saw the mission as a means of acculturating and pacifying fiercely independent peoples. The religious considered the mission as the only reliable stepping stone to salvation. The Indian saw the mission as a tolerable, if threatening, means to enter a new way of life. In other words, the mission was a complex social reality serving multiple purposes and perceived according to very different scales of value.

Some generalizations about Spanish missions are valid. In the case of the Jesuit missions there was a relatively consistent plan of organization and administration. All New Spain constituted a single, religious "province" which came under the jurisdiction of a single superior or "Provincial." Every member of the Society in New Spain was subject to his authority. For reasons of administrative, as well as religious asceticism, an individual Jesuit also answered to a local superior or "Rector." Frequently interposed between the Provincial and the Rector was a "Visitor" who held limited, delegated powers from the Provincial; this bridged the geographic gap between Mexico City and the far flung frontiers. Contrary to popular opinion, a missionary 2000 kilometers from Mexico City was not free to act independently. Even expeditions into neighboring lands required prior, explicit permission from the Provincial or the Visitor. Hence the chain of command in the Jesuit missions began with the missionary on the frontier who answered to the local Rector; the Rector, to the Visitor, and through the Visitor to the Provincial; the Provincial answered directly to the General of the Society in Rome, and in civil matters to the Viceroy.

San Xavier del Bac

The entire missionary sector was divided into "rectorates" that were responsible for clusters of missions. A particular mission often consisted of a "cabecera" or resident headquarters and several near-by "visitas" or mission stations – the distinction normally being in the residency status of a missionary. A rectorate, in turn, comprised several cabeceras. In this way the whole of northwestern New Spain's Jesuit missions were organized.

When Padre Kino came to the northwestern frontier of New Spain in 1687, he was building on the reputation and hard work of a half century of predecessors. His Blackrobe companions chose the site of Cosari for the new cabecera among the Pimas Altos. This new conversion was nothing more than the next stage in a long- standing plan of mission expansion. Kino did not ride in alone on horseback and dazzle the natives with linguistic prowess or magic. He rode in with well known missionaries who introduced him to the Indians, now eager to have their own resident European because they recognized from afar how the other villages had fared under Spanish dominion.

Padre Kino named his new post Nuestra Señora de los Dolores de Cosari. Although the initial name stood for only an individual mission station, it almost immediately became the cabecera of a series of small visitas, such as San Ignacio and Remedios. As acceptance of the missionary program spread rapidly through the Pimería Alta, Kino established

3

new cabeceras where other Jesuits became the resident missionaries; Dolores soon advanced to the status of a rectorate with Padre Kappus as the first local superior. And in this sense we moderns look back at the whole of the Pimería Alta and call the twenty-odd missions of the rectorate of Dolores the missions of Padre Kino. He had something to do with all of them; he was remotely in charge of all of them; but, there were several other Jesuit missionaries immediately responsible for their care and development. And many passed into the hands of Franciscans at a later date – in other words, Kino in origin, Kino in spirit, and historic in evolution.

When Padre Kino rode the Indian trails at the turn of the 18th century, he selected many existent villages as sites for future missions. On the following pages several of these sites are described in word and picture. None of the imposing Spanish colonial churches still standing today, however, were the handiwork of Padre Kino himself. The splendid buildings at San Xavier del Bac, Caborca, and Tubutama represent the last flourish of Franciscan efforts in a land they inherited from the expelled Jesuits. All of these churches were erected nearly a century after Kino had established the first missions in these wide-spread pueblos.

Less than a quarter century after Kino's death most of the proud structures he had personally built with his team of skilled craftsmen were crumbling into ruin. Twenty years of scarce man-power and neglect

N.S. de la Purísima Concepción de Caborca

brought the churches to the brink of total collapse. When a new wave of missionary replacements arrived in the 1730s, each felt as though he had to begin again. And even their churches, constructed through the middle of the century have – for the most part – all disappeared or given way to newer, sturdier structures. It is all part of the saga of life – of birth, death, and resurrection.

Actually all that remains of the personal work of Padre Kino are a few deeply protected adobes inside the walls of Cocóspera and under the mounded ruins of Remedios. Until 1990 the lonely ruins of Dolores boasted of a part of the church sacristy with traces of plaster and pigment, but in that year the mighty bulldozer scraped away all traces. Even after centuries, opposition to Kino's presence was finding adherents. His own churches were proud buildings, constructed by Indian craftsmen under his continual supervision. Now they are only sad monuments to the ravages of weather, Indian wars, revolutions, and blindly ignorant treasure hunters. The little physical trace that remains today of Padre Kino's presence will soon disappear as each year the summer rains cleanse the savage wounds of metal detectors and shovels that have surpassed the frenzied destruction of mission sites by Apaches and senseless revolutionaries. But even the inexorable forces of change and decay will never touch the persistent memory of Kino and the men who catapulted this desert into the annals of history. Whether a humble Jesuit ruin or a magnificent Franciscan monument, the sites and churches of the Pimería Alta will always be the missions of Padre Kino who propelled the original communities into history.

To the person who takes the time to visit the missions of northern Sonora and Arizona will come the realization that the finest hours of life are spent in helping those in need. These great mission churches rose up in the desert because people had learned the value of cooperation, sacrifice, and dignity. If these missions continue to fall into ruin, the tragedy will not be the loss of the buildings, but the loss of the sense of human solidarity that men like Kino developed in the desert southwest.

NUESTRA SEÑORA DE LOS DOLORES

Dolores, mother mission of the Pimería Alta, was founded on March 13, 1687, when Padre Eusebio Kino decided to base his apostolic ministries at the Pima village of Cosari. The site of Dolores was a favorite ranchería among the Pimas, and under the guidance of skillful missionaries it promised to yield even greater returns. Although the first mission buildings were temporary, by 1693 there was a "good and roomy church with seven bells, well provided with vestments, linens, and altars; a water-powered mill, a carpentry shop, blacksmith shop, herds of cattle and oxen, horses, a farm, orchards, vineyards, and a winery."

Memorial cross for 300th anniversary of Kino's arrival

Despite this prolific effort Kino's interest and familiarity with other regions of the Pimería deterred him from making Dolores a permanent headquarters. His major efforts at construction were focused on more remote sites along the frontier, such as Caborca and Bac. Dolores was destined to return to the dust. Only ten years after Kino's death Jesuit reports speak of Dolores as unhealthful, humid, and cold; the church was falling to the ground. Many Indians had moved away and during the ensuing decade many of those who stayed died in recurrent epidemics.

By 1732 the mission was all but abandoned; too few people were living there to warrant restoration. The last resident priest was José Javier Molina who struggled valiantly to protect the Indian population from the dreaded smallpox epidemic. Then, Padre Visitador Jean Baptiste Duquesney noted in 1744 that the mission had been vacated.

The population of the San Miguel and Cocóspera river valleys had declined so drastically by 1748 that Padre Ignacio Keller consolidated the survivors at Cocóspera where he could serve them from his own station at Santa María Suamca. The decline progressed so rapidly that Dolores was only partly inhabited by 1750, formally abandoned in 1762, and defunct, for all intents and purposes, by 1763.

Dolores cemetery in nave of Kino's mission

Wandering Spanish colonials settled in the mission ruins during the later Jesuit period. They converted some of its buildings to new uses, and by the time the Pimería Alta came into the hands of the Franciscans, the buildings and lands had been made into a hacienda.

All that remains of Dolores today is the magnificent setting and a cemetery in the fallen nave – a melancholy; reminder of the glory that has vanished from the Sorrowful Mother of the Pimería Alta.

Nuestra Señora de los Remedios

Remedios, of all Kino's missions, was the reluctant one. No sooner had Padre Kino visited the village of Coágibubig in 1687 than the Pimas living there reneged on their acceptance of building a mission. But the padre's persuasive powers won out and within seven years a large church and living quarters were under construction. The mission compound rose in slow agony; the records continually refer to the church and quarters at Remedios as "nearly completed" for four more years.

By 1699 the walls were up and the roofing was to be begun, but torrential rains eroded the apse, soaked the adobe foundations and washed out the presbytery. The damage notwithstanding, the building was repaired, and in a few months the small church was useable. Once the initial structures were completed, Kino commenced work on two large and spacious churches, here at Remedios and at Cocóspera. Both churches reached completion at the same time and Padre Kino planned a whole week of celebrations to dedicate the two churches in January, 1704. With a few minor exceptions they were architectural reflections of one another. "Each church has a high cupola set on the arches of the two chapels which form the transept, and each cupola has a sightly lantern above and in the middle."

Remedios' sanctuary wall in 1967

Unfortunately, both missions were built within range of frequent Apache raiding. Defense towers were added to the churches but these failed to protect the missions from the enemy's destructive attacks. After Kino's time the pueblo of Remedios dwindled in size and importance. Epidemics took their toll along with Apache arrows. The church was crumbling in 1723, in ruins by 1730, and totally abandoned before 1740.

Ruins of Cocóspera, Remedios' twin at the time of construction

Unlike Dolores over the rise to the south, Remedios never even became spoils for a future hacienda – everything of importance was gone. Even the vestments and church ornaments were transferred to Santa María Suamca for safe-keeping while a new mission was prepared among the Sobaipuris in the north.

Remedios is but a memory and a name which belongs to the hills surrounding it. The splendor of its church lives on only by comparing it to the decimated ruins of Cocóspera, its twin in construction and its survivor through time.

Nuestra Señora del Pilar y Santiago de Cocóspera

No church in northern Sonora has ever held the same degree of fascination created by the lonely ruin of Cocóspera. Situated on a high bluff above the picturesque Cocóspera valley, this mission has witnessed the rise and fall of empire. Apaches used the valley as a convenient route of invasion into the central Pimería. Recognizing the region as a natural staging area for defensive forays along the frontier, the Spaniards used it as a jumping off place for explorations. Its rich river lands provided the colonial residents with abundant produce, and the settlers, in turn, offered the numerous services and skills so precious to frontier life from the pueblo which grew up around the mission. After the collapse of Spanish imperial power the deserted mission-town became the home for remnants of French and American adventurers whose invasions of Sonora during the turbulent 1800's failed. Although a small town flourished here in the mid 1800s, it disappeared when travel north ceased to follow the river valleys and shifted to the lower route of the Guaymas-Tucson railroad.

The original church was the near twin of Remedios mission. Padre

Cocóspera's sanctuary pockmarked by treasure hunters

Kino laid the foundations for a large church with transepts and adobe arches. The inner walls of the ruin show clearly that the Franciscans built their church around the ruined shell of the Jesuit mission so frequently ravaged by Apache attacks. The facade of the Kino church was flanked by large, square defense towers which later formed the bases for twin bell towers. The windows and doors were constructed of posts and lintels with flat

Rubble below choir loft and main door

surfaced splays and wood-grill apertures. The interior walls were coated with a thin white plaster and decorated with red ocher paintings.

When the Franciscans renovated the mission in the late 18th century, they lined the adobe shell with fired bricks, raised strong, rock buttresses outside the nave, and erected a new brick and stucco facade. The church interior was faced with brick and heavily plastered, thus permitting an exuberance of raised plaster reliefs incorporating a variety of swags, urns, and scallop shells.

The mission ruin of Cocóspera is easily reached today by taking the Highway 2 from Imuris to Cananea. The site is located on the northwest side of the road. Perhaps it is too accessible because it has been continually ravaged by misguided treasure hunters whose pick-hammers and shovels have almost destroyed this monument to man and God on the desert frontier. For many years now the Mexican government has provided a caretaker to guard the ruins; who knows but one day lonely Cocóspera will be escorted to a new life by restoration?

SAN IGNACIO DE CABURICA

San Ignacio de Caburica, six miles up river from Magdalena de Kino, rests peacefully near some low hills around which the river veers on its southwesterly course from Imuris. San Ignacio is one of the true delights of the Sonoran mission frontier. In modern times the mission and village have been all but forgotten in the rush of business and travel.

San Ignacio, Kino's second mission

The mission site was chosen by Padre Kino in 1687 because Caburica was a populous Piman rancheria. A series of small chapels served as visitas or as temporary buildings until 1693 when Padre Agustín de Campos arrived to transform Caburica into a cabecera. His new church was burned during the Pima uprising of 1695, but soon rebuilt. For forty-three years San Ignacio served as the headquarters for Padre Campos, one of the longest terms of missionary service on record in the Pimería Alta. Quite understandably San Ignacio captured Campos' heart because of its central location and agreeable climate.

Campos' longevity and missionary skills made San Ignacio a training ground for new Jesuits moving into the missions of the Pimería.

Baroque door

Highly skilled in the various Piman dialects, his presence at San Ignacio naturally turned it into a language school and proving ground for those who would be assigned to other more distant churches. After Campos left in 1736, Padre Gaspar Stiger filled the same role of teacher and superior until his death in 1762.

Although the rector of the missions did not always reside at San Ignacio, the Pimería Alta was effectively administered from this location throughout the post-Kino period, or roughly until the expulsion of the Jesuits in 1767. The early years of Franciscan administration were dominated by the centrality of this mission, but as westward expansion overtook the Pimería, San Ignacio deferred to the more northerly and westerly missions of San Xavier del Bac, San Pedro y Pablo del Tubutama and La Concepción de Caborca. When the whole northern frontier was consolidated into the diocese of Sonora in 1779, San Ignacio drifted into oblivion. Today the pueblo is a jewel of tranquillity.

No thorough architectural investigation of San Ignacio has ever been carried out, but evidence indicates that the present church is reminiscent of the style employed by the Jesuits in the Pimería. Padre Stiger built a completely new church here in 1753, and church records imply that this structure was merely renovated and remodeled in subsequent years. Both Franciscan and secular

Caracol stairs

priests undertook extensive remodeling, but comparative study shows that the bell tower, size of the nave, and the circular, mesquite-log staircase were characteristic of the earlier churches of the Pimería.

13

SAN PEDRO Y SAN PABLO DEL TUBUTAMA

A visit to Tubutama is to relive the missionary past – but without missionaries. Although the pueblo is well off the main highway, it is accessible by paved roads. From any angle of approach the town looms up like a welcome oasis in the desert, dominated by the squared towers of a white mission church. The church fronts on a plaza that is frequently void of cars or trucks; usually one or two horses stand in the shade of local cantinas. A pervading silence is broken occasionally by the voices of children at play or by a burro train clopping through the streets.

In 1687 Padre Kino was invited to Tubutama. Immediately, he began construction on a small church and mission visita. The struggling new mission was later the scene of the outbreak of the Pima rebellion of 1695. The mission itself was burned out and the crops destroyed. But it was only a short while before the repentant Indians repaired the damage and Tubutama took its quiet place in the history of the Pimería. As isolated as the town now seems, Tubutama served as the jumping off station for the bold crossings of the Papaguería that had to be undertaken to explore the western deserts.

Tubutama before restoration

Tubutama, old interior

After Kino's time manpower was at a premium and Tubutama only occasionally and temporarily had a resident priest. By 1730, however, more men were sent as missionaries into the Pimería, and Tubutama was raised to the level of a cabecera at which time a new church was erected. Padre Jacob Sedelmayr, another famous Jesuit explorer, built a church here at mid-century. But it came to grief during the 1751 Pima rebellion when Luis of Sáric burned the church and murdered several residents of the pueblo. Once the rebellion was quelled the church was again rebuilt; a decent structure was reported here by Padre Manuel Aguirre in 1764.

When the Franciscans took over in 1768, the mission enjoyed a favored place in the Pimería and a new, more elaborate church was built here in 1788. This is the same structure that graces the pueblo today. Recent repair and restoration have paid strict attention to the earliest known details so that the church today remains a fine example of what it once was. The older mission buildings were apparently closer to the river bluff than the present church, but all trace of them has disappeared. In the early 1950s a group of American adventurers, searching for the fictitious Jesuit treasure, nearly dynamited the pueblo. Fortunately the men were stopped in time or another masterpiece of colonial architecture would have crumbled in tragic ruin.

Another stunning change at Tubutama was the construction of Cuatemoc Reservoir, damming up the ever flowing Altar River where mission fields once flowered.

San Antonio del Oquitoa

Arriving in Altar, one never gets the impression it was at the junction of two major Sonoran rivers. Irrigation projects and deep water wells have so altered the flow of water that only a wary traveler would suspect how the terrain looked in colonial times. The nearest village up river from Altar is the quaint community of San Antonio del Oquitoa. A

San Antonio de Oquitoa

simple, lonely church surmounts a rounded hill above the town; its stark lines are surrounded by a sun-seared cemetery.

Oquitoa was never an important historical site even in Padre Kino's day. What fame it had was infamous because residents of this town were the murderers of Padre Saeta in Caborca. But now Oquitoa has taken its quiet place in history and has become a favored spot along the Kino mission trail.

In 1980 restoration work was completed on the then decaying church. Fascinating discoveries were made of earlier construction techniques and decorative details. Now San Antonio del Oquitoa has taken a position of pride in the history of Sonora. The narrow nave, thick adobe walls, and beam ceiling remain as one of the last vestiges of a truly bygone era. Oquitoa doesn't seem very different today from what it must have been in the 18th century.

Rarely in Jesuit mission country does one encounter a church under the patronage of Franciscan saints. In the case of San Antonio del Oquitoa it appears that the patron of the village was chosen because the first resident priest in the Altar valley was Padre Antonio Arias at Tubutama. Soon after his appointment Oquitoa became a visita in his care. It is curious how strongly history is written in the traces of unassuming names.

SAN DIEGO DEL PITIQUITO

In the days of Padre Kino, Pitiquito was never a very important pueblo although he frequently visited there. For years it remained a dependent mission station of Caborca. In 1772 Fray Antonio de los Reyes, later the first bishop of Sonora, reported that there was no church at the site. The Franciscans began the present structure in 1778; since then, the church has undergone extensive modification.

The history of Pitiquito has been vague at best. In the early months of 1967 the residents of the town became terrified at what they thought were the appearances of spirits in the church. Skeletons, eyes, hands, and words emerged and vanished on the massive white-washed walls throughout the interior of the church. The more timorous people interpreted these words and figures as omens predicting the immediate end of the world.

But on investigation it was found that the ladies of the town had been cleaning the church for a fiesta. They used detergents to wash the walls. And a day or so after each cleansing, figures and words would appear on the surface. What no one knew is that the whole church had been decorated with large liturgical and doctrinal murals, but the paintings are so old that not even the oldest resident had the faintest recollection of ever seeing the church with anything but a

San Diego del Pitiquito

white-washed interior. A request has been made to the Mexican federal government to attempt to restore the murals since they could well become the best example of catechetical art known for this period of Sonoran history.

La Purísima Concepción de Nuestra Señora de Caborca

Deceptively peaceful, Caborca rises along the banks of the Río Concepción at the heart of an amazingly fertile plain in the great western desert of Sonora. Padre Kino himself was impressed by its potential and began constructing a new mission here in 1693. He entrusted his hopes for the mission's future to Padre Francisco Xavier Saeta, but the Pima rebellion of 1695 demolished those hopes with the murder of Saeta and the pillaging of the village. Caborca, however, recovered and for a half century grew in importance as the western staging area for explorations into the Colorado delta.

But Caborca's calm was shattered again in the Pima rebellion of 1751; this time the blood of Padre Tomás Tello stained the sands of the agricultural heartland. Again peace returned to the broad valley and the agricultural economy pulsed with new importance. Although one might suspect that such an isolated place would eventually experience peace, it did not; violence broke out in 1857 when Henry A. Crabb and his filibuster army besieged the townspeople in the mission church. His ill-fated attempt to seize northern Sonora ended in the execution of his entire force on the mission steps. Residents claim that the bullet marks on the facade date from this historical episode.

The present church was built between 1803 and 1809. It shows many architectural similarities to San Xavier del Bac. A large convento once stood to the north of the church but raging floods in the early 20th century ripped into this construction and also eroded away the sacristy and rear of the sanctuary; it happened again in the 1980s.

The Mexican government has since restored the church and made it a national monument. Caborca is less remembered for being an important mission and the scene of two martyrdoms than for its being the place where American expansion into Mexico was halted by the bullets of Sonoran patriots.

A new plaza was created in front of the church in 1967. The small archway which serves as the formal entrance to the plaza was made from the stone facade of an ancient chapel in the town of Batuc which has been inundated by the waters of El Novillo dam on the Río Yaqui. In 1997 the plaza was greatly expanded.

SAN CAYETANO DEL TUMACÁCORI

Tumacácori's past is elusive. All the maps of Padre Kino indicate an Indian village of Tumacácori on the east bank of the Santa Cruz River. Apparently the site was a convenient crossing place where the waters of the river had a chance to broaden out. From Tumacácori the trail crossed the river to the west and continued on down to San Xavier del Bac. Actually the Pima settlement of Tumacácori gained importance only after the establishment of the presidio of Tubac in 1752. Prior to this, the main concentration of Indians was at Los Angeles de Guevavi, an extensive mission some twelve miles up river. In many ways the early history of Tumacácori is the history of Guevavi. Guevavi, like Tumacácori, was an original Kino visita, but a major mission complex was not built here until

Aerial view of Tumacácori showing granary and mortuary chapel

after Kino's time, in 1732 when Padre Johann Grazhofer took charge.

Exactly ten miles south of Tumacácori was also located the mission visita of Calabasas. Throughout Jesuit times there was nothing more here than a small wayside chapel, and its importance varied with the shifts in Indian population. It seems that because of recurrent Apache raids the Sobaipuris pulled out of the San Pedro river valley and took refuge at these missions within the sphere of Spanish protection.

Since the present mission bears a different name, San José de Tumacácori, than the one Kino chose, it is most probable that the church was erected on a new and somewhat different site from that of Kino's. Archaeological investigation has revealed a structure immediately east of the present church and most probably represents a Jesuit period church that enjoyed protection from the Tubac presidio (after 1752). The present mission was erected in 1773 and refurbished at various times. Construction on a larger church was begun in the opening years of the Mexican War for Independence and suspended in 1822 due to the lack of funds from royal coffers. Nevertheless, the church remained in use until secularization became fully effective in the 1840's. Mexican utilization of the property for mining activities gave rise to later American speculation that the mission was the scene of clandestine mining by Catholic clerics.

Tumacácori is now the headquarters for the Tumacácori National Historical Park. The site originally came under Park Service control in 1908 when it was made a National Monument; and it was raised to full park status by an act of Congress in 1990.

Los Santos Angeles de Guevavi

Situated on the Guevavi Ranch on the east bank of the Río Santa Cruz are the last traces of Arizona's oldest Jesuit mission, Los Santos Angeles de Guevavi. The site was selected by Padre Kino in the early 1690s because of its centrality to the scattered rancherias of the upper river valley. Through the first years of its existence it was known variously as San Raphael Archangel, San Gabriel Archangel, and finally as Los Santos Angeles; no one could remember which patron was foremost anymore. Its first resident missionary was Padre Juan de San Martín who arrived in 1701; but the mission was soon abandoned and not until 1732 did Guevavi again host a resident priest.

Guevavi circa 1960

Although reconstructed after the ravages of the 1751 Pima rebellion, Guevavi's fortunes waned and by the last quarter of the 18th century it was reduced to a visita – often exposed to Apache raids and too far from protection by the garrison at Tubac. Graves of several prominent Sonorans, as the wife of Juan Bautista de Anza, were located in the nave, but all have been destroyed by avid treasure hunters. The National Park Service now has custody of the site.

The Visitas of the San Pedro, Santa María and Altar Rivers

Curiously the most scenic sections of the Sonoran border are rarely seen by tourists or even residents of the region. The natural causeways of communication in colonial times were the river valleys that are now avoided by modern transportation. Hence the splendors known so well to the men who made history in the Pimería Alta are enigmas to us who have come so suddenly upon the complex past. We travel different trails in faster vehicles along topographically altered highways.

The lower reaches of the Río San Pedro were studded with short-lived rancherias and potential visitas. The Apache menace drove the Sobaipuri Pimas from their traditional homes and eliminated the potential for conversion. To the west over the Huachuca Mountains, the upper portion of the Río Santa María (now the Río Santa Cruz) boasted a cabecera at Santa María Suamca (near Lochiel) and visitas at San Lazaro and San Luis Bacoancos. But a furious attack in 1768 obliterated the village and mission at Suamca. Then, the weakened condition of the Opata-Sobaipuri villages contributed to the collapse of the defensive perimeter along the Pimería Alta frontier. Over exposed and under staffed, garrisons at Terrenate, Tubac, and Altar were unable secure the frontier

Visitas along the Altar River present a similar history. Some of the them along this reliable water course rose to full mission status only to fall back again into ruin. A case in point is Santa Theresa de Atil, or Adid. Whatever the proprieties of the name, the place was made famous by Padre Ignaz Pfefferkorn in his classic *Description of Sonora*. When Pfefferkorn worked there in 1756, traces of the Kino chapel were still visible because the place had been by-passed in the rebellion of '51. Atil fell on hard times after Pfefferkorn was transferred to Cucurpe. Apaches raided it frequently; missionaries refused to minister to its flock, and eventually the vestments and church furnishings were lost.

Farther up the Río Altar, the important town of Sáric, was a mission for a short while. Now the people dispute where the mission might have been because its last vestiges have been so badly mistreated and forgotten. The same goes for Tucubavia, Búsanic, and other ephemeral villages along the ancient riverway.

SAN XAVIER DEL BAC

The foundations for the great mission of San Xavier del Bac were laid in 1700 by Padre Eusebio Kino. He had been impressed some years before by this largest of the Pima villages along the Santa Cruz. But even after the mission was completed, it remained vacant throughout the first decades of the 18th century. The first resident missionary Padre Francisco Gonzalvo fell terribly ill and died of pneumonia at San Ignacio the following August, 1702. With the shortage of missionaries in the north-

Facade of San Xavier del Bac

west, Bac remained vacant until 1732 when the Swiss nobleman, Philip Segesser attempted to re-gain lost ground. Even Segesser's stay was brief because he had to leave to care for his companion, Padre Grazhofer, who was deathly ill at Guevavi. With Grazhofer's death in 1733, Segesser split his time between the two missions. But illness felled him as well and Bac was taken over by yet another Swiss missionary, Padre Gaspar Stiger. Stiger stayed until 1737 when he moved south to replace the elderly Padre Campos at San Ignacio. San Xavier del Bac was then turned over to José Torres Perea, who lasted for two years until 1741. The isolation and distance from Spanish assistance made the post particularly difficult and dangerous.

The sequence of mission churches at Bac has long been disputed because of the incompleteness of the record. Kino's first church was be-gun here in April, 1700, and he monitored its construction throughout the first decade of the 1700s. Whether completed or not, no church was reported here in the 1720s. It would appear, however, that some edifice served as a church during the residency of Segesser, Stiger, Torres Perea, and Francisco Paver, who arrived in 1750 just prior to the Pima Revolt of 1751. During that ominous time the mission of San Xavier was pillaged and burned.

Bishop Granjon's entry gate from Tucson

Following an interlude of a couple of years, Padre Paver tried his luck again at Bac. He was back in 1753, but he determined it was wiser to operate out of Guevavi where there were still remnants of a mission. In late 1755 Padre Alonso Espinosa, a native of the Canary islands and recent missionary at Caborca, was transferred to Bac. He came in the auspicious company of the new Governor of Sonora, Antonio de Mendoza. While campaigning in the north in 1756, Mendoza stopped off at San Xavier to lay the cornerstone of a new and capacious church, which Espinosa worked on over the next several years. The foundations of this historic building lie forty yards west of the present church.

St. Francis Xavier

Espinosa's large adobe structure was the same one utilized by the Franciscans when they took over in 1768 from the exiled Jesuits. It served as headquarters for Fray Francisco Hermenigildo Garcés until he was transferred to Tucson to be in close support for the newly constructed presidio. In 1777 San Xavier was placed in the hands of Fray Juan Bautista Velderrain, who looked after the mission while Garcés explored routes to Alta California.

Bac's history has always been fascinating because it has always housed the largest Indian populations. For centuries it has been the meeting place and training ground for the hechiceros, medicine men, of neighboring tribes. From here Kino sent out messengers to learn about the peculiar blue shells which figured so prominently in the discovery that California was not an island. Kino dreamed of moving his headquarters to Bac, but the lack of men to assume responsibilities at Dolores made the move impossible.

Today, mission San Xavier del Bac is one of the colonial art treasures of America. Its baroque architecture is a monument to the splendor of the European civilization that first came to the desert frontier of Sonora and Arizona. Surrounded by fields of grain and cotton and by the adobe dwellings of the Papagos, it is a page from the past that has been forgotten in the haste of freeways and the waste of crowded cities.

THE MISSIONS OF THE LOWER GILA AND COLORADO RIVERS

The Indian pueblos along the Gila bore a litany of apostolic names but to call them missions is to raise them to a dignity beyond the reality. At most, they were visitas for the missionaries of San Xavier del Bac, San Pedro del Tubutama, Santa María Suamca, and Los Angeles de Guevavi. Yet they have been traditionally so de-emphasized that their existence as visitas has been overlooked.

From the time of Padre Kino these pueblos were considered as potential missions and were to be visited whenever possible. Mission maps for the entire first half of the 1700s depict the chain of villages. There was continual contact, first with Kino, then Campos, and down through the years by Padres Ignacio Keller, Jacob Sedelmayr, and quite probably Gaspar Stiger and Alonso Espinosa. They were certainly attended by the Franciscans, most notably Fray Francisco Garcés.

It is nearly impossible to imagine the meaning of the Gila and Colorado missions today. The villages and their Indian populations have long since disappeared just as the shallow-draft steamers that once plied the desert river waters. But in the days of the active missions of the Pimería they were outposts on a frontier that strained toward California, the last havens of supply for the men who were penetrating the "Moqui" lands to the north and west.

The central pueblo along this coveted chain was San Dionisio, roughly identifiable with present day Yuma. The melodious Christian names of villages that ran upstream from San Dionisio are gone; San Pedro and Pablo, San Thadeo and San Simón have given way to Dome and Wellton. Thus the modern American frontier has erased any memory of these ancient sites where the Gila Pimas and Cocomaricopas met the Cross and Crown.

The shorter chain of missions down the Colorado among the Yuman peoples bore the names of the patrons of Spanish royalty – Santa Isabel, San Félix de Valois, San Casimiro. But none of these pueblos reached any significant level of development until long after the Jesuit expulsion in 1767. In the last quarter of the eighteenth century the misguided policies of Teodoro de Croix, the governor of the northern provinces, spelled an end to the missionary hopes enkindled here by Padres Kino and Campos.

De Croix's policies were a direct attack on the mission system. He wanted instant integration which amounted to sudden slavery for the Indians along the Colorado. Fray Francisco Garcés, O.F.M. tried valiantly to continue the expansion of the missions, but his policies crumpled under the "enlightened" guidance of De Croix. The Indians of the Colorado saw clearly through the Spanish colonial plan for them. So they rose in revolt in July, 1781, massacring some fifty Spaniards including Fray Garcés and Captain Fernando Rivera y Moncada, the military commander of Baja California.

The Jesuit visitas along the Colorado by then had disappeared with the shift of Indian population centers, and the Franciscan missions were now burned to the ground. The Yuman nation maintained stiff resistance to Spanish conquest and the mission system never revived in the river delta.

The falling facade of Cocóspera

THE MISSIONS AS OTHERS SAW THEM

BY THOMAS H. NAYLOR

The buildings that today comprise the "Kino chain of missions" stand witness to the inexorable forces of time. Whether from neglect or abandonment to the harsh physical forces of the Sonoran Desert, or due to a royal decision from Madrid to exile and replace an entire religious order with another, the churches have under-gone rebuilding and continual change. While some of the monuments have slowly eroded back into the earth, most of the buildings have seen periods of reconstruction and remodeling – right up to the present day.

Each church is unique as to its community setting, particular history, and the amount of interest and concern it has been shown. Lacking a protective community to care for it, Cocóspera has been ravaged by man and the elements to a near formless ruin. Only very recently has it been given any protection. Other Pimería churches have succumbed entirely. San Ignacio, Oquitoa and Tubutama have always enjoyed the care and protection of the small but immensely proud villages nestled at their feet. Shunted aside in the wake of the agro-boom, Caborca's mission church nearly fell total victim to flood erosion. Rescued because of its nationalistic importance as the scene of a Mexican victory over invading *norteamericanos*, the lost sections have now been rebuilt; the restored church and convento appear on the way to becoming a museum.

San Xavier del Bac found itself in the United States after 1853. That fact, and its proximity to heavily traveled routes in and out of Tucson, placed it in the limelight. Subsequently, a succession of church funded projects and state and federal assistance has beautifully preserved it. Being the finest example of Spanish colonial architecture in the U.S. has not hurt San Xavier. Both Tumacácori and Guevavi, also in Arizona, have fared much worse. Considerably less impressive and already in varying states of ruin, Tumacácori was eventually saved from oblivion by the National Park Service, but only mounds and fragments of walls mark the site of Guevavi today.

The visual record of the Pimería churches begins in the middle of the 19th century in the form of drawings and sketches. Among the best are those of J. Ross Browne in 1864 and Alphonse Pinart in 1879, examples of which appear in the following pages. The earliest photographs date from the 1870s and are relatively plentiful after 1900. Their quality and condition vary considerably. In the views that follow every attempt was made to include those that were most skillfully made and which most dramatically document the ever-changing churches through time.

SAN XAVIER DEL BAC

Taken probably in 1884, this view by H.T. Watkins shows the mortuary chapel and wall intact. Only two of the *estipite* columns have fallen from the portal decoration. *Courtesy of the Arizona State Museum*

View from "Grotto" Hill prior to the 1887 earthquake.
Courtesy Arizona State Museum

The mission restored and landscaped circa 1950.
Courtesy Arizona State Museum

"San Francisco" in west chapel before restoration

SAN JOSÉ DE TUMACÁCORI

J. Ross Browne drew this somewhat exaggerated sketch in 1864.
From *Adventures in Apache Country*

Taken sometime around 1913, the photo shows the attic above the
facade fallen. The roof was restored to the nave in 1920.
Robert Forbes, Arizona Historical Society

San Ignacio de Caburica

Dimwiddie posed people in front of
cemetery wall in 1894.
Courtesy of Smithsonian Institution

Side altars have
statues from old chapel
in Magdalena

Artifacts dating back
to 1683 are guarded
in a small musuem.

Santa María Magdalena

J. Ross Browne's 1884 sketch shows the present church
and Campos' chapel apparently toward the right.

The sketch by Alphonse Pinart in 1871 distinctly shows the Campos'
chapel in front of and to the right of the present church.

An unidentified photographer took this photo around 1900 showing
the *espedaña* and *estipites* missing from the facade.
(perhaps due to earthquake damage in 1887?)
Courtesy Southwest Museum, Los Angeles

Courtesy Southwest Museum, Los Angeles

San Pedro y Pablo de Tubutama

An unknown photographer took this photo around 1900 showing a weathered church and barren plaza. Note the two small towers over the facade which were removed shortly afterwards.
Courtesy Arizona State Museum

Note attempt to imitate marble cornices with vegetal painting. Taken in 1935, the church was stripped of furnishings for protection against anti-clerical desecration.
Grant, Western Archaeological Center

SAN ANTONIO DE OQUITOA

The haunting church and cemetery on the hill above Oquitoa were thoroughly restored in the 1980s.

Interior showing mesquite beam ceiling and ocotilla cross ribs.
Courtesy Western Archaeological Center

La Purísima Concepción de Caborca

Much of the convento was still intact until floods in 1908 tore them away. The architecture is very similar to San Xavier del Bac.
Courtesy Arizona State Museum

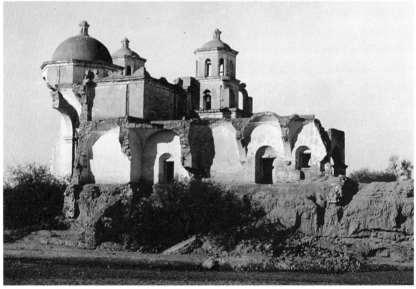

Located at the bend of the Río Concepción, the mission has been repeatedly damaged in successive floods through the 1980s.

Severe damage to sanctuary prior to restoration

THE DISCOVERY OF PADRE KINO'S GRAVE

From time immemorial history has explained the monuments of man's changing achievements. But in modern times man achieves change so rapidly that his links to the past are lost in the pace of change itself. History is no longer enough. So in recent decades man has developed the skill to search the ruins of his past to bring greater meaning to his present. The science of archaeology and the art of history have become as significant as astronautics and bio-physics because they create the perspective of man's cultural and scientific growth.

In this way the tiny town of Magdalena de Kino in Sonora, Mexico, is as significant as Guaymas with its satellite tracking station. Here in Magdalena in May, 1966, a team of anthropologists and historians located and identified the grave of Padre Eusebio Francisco Kino. The successful discovery climaxed nearly forty years of frustrating failures to identify the grave site.

When Herbert E. Bolton, as a young historian, published his translation of *Kino's Memoirs of the Pimería Alta* in 1919, he speculated that Padre Kino's remains had been transferred to San Ignacio de Caburica. Or at least that's what the local rumor of the time held. But in the meanwhile, the burial registers of San Ignacio were discovered, and in them Padre Campos carefully recorded where he had buried Kino in the chapel of San Francisco Xavier in 1711. Apparently Bolton and Professor Frank Lockwood probed the foundations of the present church in Magdalena around 1928, hoping to find Kino's grave. At least that's how the story is told today. By the time Bolton published his renowned biography of Padre Kino, *The Rim of Christendom*, in 1936, he dropped any mention of Kino's transferal to San Ignacio. The entry that mentioned Kino's burial in the little chapel of San Francisco Xavier stood as the single, reliable record of history about his grave. But where was that grave? In fact, where was the chapel? Indeed, where was the town in 1711? Unknown to almost everyone was Bolton's own opinion. Writing to Professor Lockwood, he told him he would "walkover the Padre's grave as he approached the church of Santa María Magdalena."

Many Mexican anthropologists and historians had tried to discover the obscured grave. Serapio Dávila in 1928 undertook an extensive search. He opened trenches in front of the present church and found the cemented foundations of an old parochial structure. Soon his workers were uncovering hordes of scattered bones, part of an old cemetery. How would one ever tell Kino's grave from any other? Dávila gave up.

Through the decades of the 30's and the 40's Professor Eduardo W. Villa, Rubén Parodi, Professor Fernando Pesqueira, and Señorita Dolores Encinas devoted their talents to solve the mystery of the missing site. But each effort ended in failure. New theories and newer rumors arose to explain the failures, thus creating only more confusion. In 1961 *Arizona Highways* dedicated their March issue to Padre Eusebio Kino – 250 years after his death in Magdalena. The state of Arizona was justly proud of its pioneer padre, and the circumstances of the dedication rekindled the same perplexing question: where was Kino's grave? In a gesture toward solution Editor Raymond Carlson incorporated into the issue an article by Donald Page in collaboration with Colonel Gilbert Proctor. The article focused attention on a complex of private dwellings on Calle Pesqueira some four blocks distant from the present church. Old timers called the place, "La Capilla." Indeed the structure looked like a chapel with its arches, niches, and scalloped passageways. Beyond what he had written Donald Page could not be consulted about his reasons for thinking this was the chapel of San Francisco Xavier; Page was dead. Colonel Proctor remained firmly convinced this was the authentic site.

Former failures to find the grave and new rumors reinforced each other until the residents of Magdalena could sit idle no longer. The grave should be found! In the late spring of 1963 the Magdalena Lions' Club obtained the permission of the Villa family to excavate the rooms of their family home on Calle Pesqueira; this was the erstwhile La Capilla. Curiously, the searchers found a subterranean tile floor, broken through in three places as if a coffin and two boxes had been removed through it. The rubble from the hole contained an old shoe, some beer bottles, and a cigarette lighter, indicating the hole had probably been refilled in the late 1920's. Many interpreted this discovery as evidence for the removal of Kino's remains (for protective custody) during the religious persecution of President Calles' regime.

Olvera's conceptual drawing of the Magdalena church
and Campos' chapel

A slow, careful investigation was then begun in the summer of 1963 by the Reverend Charles Polzer, S.J., to evaluate the findings of the Lions' Club project and to sort rumor from fact. With the help of Dr. William Wasley, resident archaeologist of the Arizona State Museum, it became evident that the excavation of "Proctor's Chapel," as La Capilla came to be known, were inconclusive at best. In fact, everything pointed to this site's being wholly incorrect. If true, then Kino had never been there to be removed!

Further historical investigations were undertaken in 1964 by Father Polzer. They were conclusive: the Proctor site was false. An archaeological survey of other Kino mission sites in the Pimería further corroborated Polzer and Wasley's objections to the validity of the Proctor site. But the discovery of the unusual openings in the tile floor of the "chapel" convinced the people that Padre Kino's bones had been carried off to safety decades ago. Rumor persisted and Magdalena was a maze of conflicting opinion.

While preparations for sculpting of the Kino Memorial Statue neared completion, the search for Kino's grave was shelved. In February, 1965, the nation was introduced to the prominence of Padre Kino by the unveiling of his statue in the nation's Capitol. Little did the people responsible for the statue realize what they had wrought concerning the discovery of Kino's grave. Mexico, too, was justly proud of Padre Kino; the Mexican people were not about to forfeit their share in Kino's fame.

Hence, at the request of Mexican President Diaz Ordaz, the Secretary of Public Education, Agustín Yáñez, commissioned Professor Wigberto Jiménez Moreno, the director of the Department of Historical Investigation of the National Institute of Anthropology and History (INAH), to find the remains of Padre Kino. It was June 30, 1965. Whatever legal log-jams the Americans conjectured over in the search for Kino's grave were swept away by the executive order of the Mexican federal government. Professor Jiménez Moreno, Dr. Jorge Olvera, the colonial art historian, and Professor Arturo Romano, the physical anthropologist of the National Institute, began a systematic search of the archives for information about the grave.

A quick trip to the Sonora frontier in August, 1965, acquainted Jiménez Moreno and Olvera with their newly inherited problem. Rumors and opinions varied on all aspects: the grave, the chapel, the remains, and their transfer. Professor Jiménez Moreno retired to Mexico City profoundly aware he had more on his hands than a casual search. Dr. Olvera remained behind to begin the methodical excavations which eventually crisscrossed the site of the ancient pueblo.

The traditional Fiesta of San Francisco forced an interruption of work in October. The trenches were back-filled and the investigators took advantage of the recess to evaluate their problem. Professor Jiménez Moreno accurately reassessed the situation. The discovery of the grave and the verification of the remains of Padre Kino would be no simple matter. The ingredients of success would be men and knowledge, both archaeological and historical.

It was April, 1966, when the team arrived again in Magdalena. Jiménez Moreno invited other qualified investigators to join the team. Padre Cruz Acuña from Hermosillo pitched in to comb through old diocesan archives and to interview old timers. The Reverend Kieran McCarty, O.F.M., historian of San Xavier del Bac (Tucson), signed on as research historian; his familiarity with Franciscan records aided materially in piecing out the fate of the old chapel. Dr. William Wasley was placed on detached service from the Arizona State Museum; his keen knowledge of the archaeology of the region provided the team with essential knowledge and skills. The chemist from the local clinic, Dr. Gabriel Sánchez de la Vega, gave invaluable service as the man most acquainted with the recent attempts to find the grave.

To the men of Mexico City in 1965 the search for the grave of Padre Kino appeared to be a simple matter. To the same men on the scene in Magdalena in 1966 the search was recognized as enormously complicated, and perhaps impossible. Excitement charged the air of Magdalena as the experts challenged the unknown.

Professor Jiménez Moreno understood his problem well. Here was a situation that required solution by a process of elimination. Units of the team spread out from Magdalena to probe each site favored by certain rumors and opinions. No reasonable possibility ·was overlooked, but one by one they were being eliminated as archaeological and historical evidence piled up. Slowly the circle of probability narrowed to

The team confirms the discovery, May 1966:
L to R: P. Santos Saenz, W.W. Wasley, Jiménez Moreno, J. Olvera, J. Matiella, and E. Burrus, S.J. Not shown; P. Kieran McCarty, OFM, A. Romano, and G. Sánchez de la Vega.

the plaza in front of the Magdalena church. Over two kilometers of exploratory trenches wandered through the town. Work crews exposed foundations of buildings long since forgotten. The earth yielded the bones of countless human beings.

It seemed as though the search would succumb to the intricacies of its own method. Then, the breaks began to come. The historians were building up key clues about the chapel from the archives. The major find was a description of the little chapel of San Francisco Xavier in an 1828 report by don Fernando Grande:

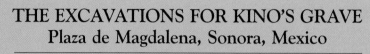

THE EXCAVATIONS FOR KINO'S GRAVE
Plaza de Magdalena, Sonora, Mexico

MAP LEGEND

1 Padre Eusebio Francisco Kino, buried 1711
2 Padre Manuel Gonzales, reburied 1712
3 Padre Ignacio Iturmendi, reburied 1712
4 Salvador de Noriega, buried 1739
5 José Gabriel Vega, buried 1837

Areas Excavated
Older Building Foundations
Present Buildings, (1966)
portions razed in 1967

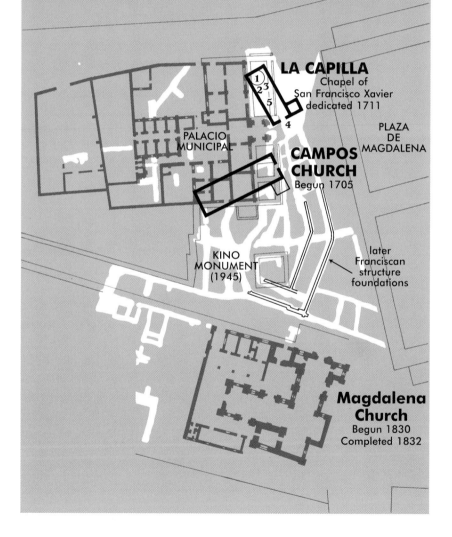

LA CAPILLA
Chapel of
San Francisco Xavier
dedicated 1711

PLAZA
DE
MAGDALENA

PALACIO
MUNICIPAL

CAMPOS
CHURCH
Begun 1705

KINO
MONUMENT
(1945)

later
Franciscan
structure
foundations

Magdalena
Church
Begun 1830
Completed 1832

The chapel of this town is moderate. It is of adobe material. The entrance faces south. There is a moderate little tower in which are located three bells and another small one. It has nothing that draws particular attention. The principal and only altar is in the chancel. On it are set an image of the crucified Christ and another of the Virgin of Dolores; at the feet of the larger carving is the littler one of ordinary quality. And in some niches which form a reredos along the wall of the altar are set the statue of St. Magdalene, the patron of the pueblo (it's small but well carved), one of St. Francis Xavier, and one of Blessed Joseph Oriol; the latter is imperfectly carved. Midway in the nave of the church is a niche where there is located in a case a large carving of St. Francis Xavier, an object of devotion everywhere in the northwest. It is a beautiful and serious sculpture.

From the burial register two more relevant facts were learned. In 1739 a Spaniard, Salvador de Noriega, was buried at the entrance to the chapel. Nearly a century later a ninety year old Indian resident, José Gabriel Vega, was buried before the niche of St. Francis Xavier.

While the historians read through miles of micro film and dusted off old records, the archaeological teams followed the clues exposed by their trenching. The cement foundations in front of the church which had occupied Dávila years before were soon discounted when it was learned that lime was not used for construction in the Pimería during the earlier Jesuit period. Traces of adobe walls became more evident as the work crews learned the difficult art of distinguishing an adobe foundation from the alluvial deposits natural to the terrain. One wall which ran east and west had attracted the attention of Dr. Olvera who felt that it maintained the proper orientation shown in some mid-19th century sketches of the pueblo. But what is one wall in the middle of a whole town?

Dr. Wasley convinced the team of the need to correlate their findings with known Jesuit ruins in the Pimería; this was a stratagem worked out a year before between Wasley and Polzer, who insisted on the utility of the uncontaminated ruins at Remedios. On the very day Wasley, Olvera, and Romano were making their reconnaissance, the workmen in the trench that followed Olvera's favored wall came to its end. Professor Jiménez saw that they had really reached a corner. The wall turned toward the

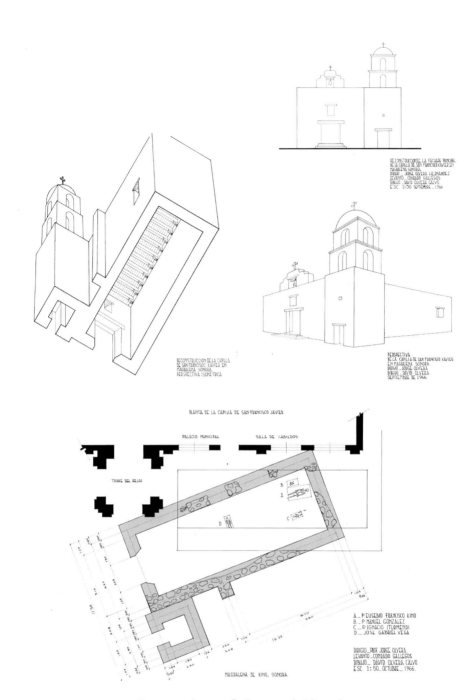

Perspectives of Campos' Church.

50

City Hall. This was the first clear indication that it might define the foundations of a building.

Earlier in the exploration a crew had followed a lateral trench from Olvera's wall. Close to the north-south axis of the main trench they exposed a skeleton which Professor Romano identified as that of a European. Everyone regarded the discovery as "Suspect Number One." But then other pieces of the puzzle began to fall into place. "Suspect Number One" was on the south side of the adobe wall, and now that the long adobe wall to the east of the burial had turned a corner westward, there was little doubt that the Number One Suspect was Salvador de Noriega.

The east wall of the building showed evidence of a small buttress about midway. This corresponded to another historical discovery that Padre José Pérez Llera in 1828 erected a buttress to prevent the wall from further slumping! The corner discovered on the day the team was reconnoitering other missions proved to be that of the apse of the chapel. Cautiously the crews followed the line of the adobe and boulder foundation. The sharp spades cut through the soil ever so carefully. A shovel full of earth spewed into the screen. Nothing. Then at the base of the trench fell a piece of a skull, dislodged from the edge! A cry! Tension mounted as Dr. Wasley, Dr. Olvera, Dr. Romano and Professor Jiménez Moreno carefully exposed the whole skull. Could it be? Could it really be Kino's? It was 4:45 on the afternoon of May 19, 1966.

The entire team concentrated on the complex of trenches that seemed now to be located on the site of the ancient chapel. The skeleton discovered that fateful afternoon was delicately uncovered. The earth within the entire chapel area was cautiously peeled back. Then the key elements began to fall in place without complication. "Kino" was an original burial on the Gospel side of the chapel; the body had rested between the second and third foundation support, just as the burial record of Padre Agustín de Campos said. Then, at Kino's feet, but closer to the west wall, appeared a "secondary burial," one that had been transferred from another place. Across the chapel floor area, on the Epistle side of the apse, another secondary burial was uncovered in the packed earth. Fantastic! But predictable if this were really the chapel. In 1712, one year after Kino's burial in the chapel, Padre Campos transferred the bodies of Padres Iturmendi and González from Tubutama and interred them in the same

Fr. Polzer views Kino's remains, 1970

chapel on the Epistle and the Gospel side respectively.

Midway down the body of the church the excavators came upon another burial of a very old Indian man. Another key slipped into place because ninety year old José Gabriel Vega was buried before the niche of St. Francis Xavier which itself was located half way down the nave! And Salvador de Noriega was still lying patiently at the southerly entrance.

Professor Romano carefully studied the skeleton which lay on the gospel side of the building – if this were really the chapel. The man had been in his 60's. Kino had been 66. The skull was a classic European type from the Alpine region. Kino was from the Tyrol. The tibia bones of the legs showed a pronounced retroflexion. This was characteristic of the mountain people of Kino's homeland. When Wasley and Olvera removed the last traces of the wooden coffin which had caved in on the chest of the skeleton, they found a small bronze cross lying on the clavicle. This was typical of the Jesuit missionary of the 17th century.

On May 21, 1966, the team reached the conclusion that it had in fact discovered the long lost remains of Padre Eusebio Francisco Kino. On May 24 the announcement was made to the general public; no doubt remained in the minds of any of the team or the experts called in after the initial conclusion was reached. Rev. Ernest Burrus of the Jesuit Historical Institute at Rome, who luckily was visiting in Tucson, agreed in full. And finally on July 14, 1966, the Academy of History met in Mexico City to review the evidence. Professor Jiménez Moreno presented seventy-two depositions explaining the discovery. Then, Dr. Alberto Caso in the name of the Mexican Academy of History pronounced in favor of the

Bronze cross

identity of the remains. Padre Kino was found at last.

As with everything that man does, there are always those who doubt. Some wanted the archaeologists to uncover a plaque or headstone. None ever existed, particularly for a man like Kino. He died as he had lived, in poverty and in the presence of his Lord. What the doubters had forgotten was that the monument over his grave was not just a headstone, but a chapel, and not just a cross with a name, but a whole culture.

So conclusive is the evidence which the team under Professor Jiménez Moreno uncovered that if the skeleton had been marked with another name, the anthropologists and historians would have realized someone was trying to play a joke.

But perhaps the most remarkable thing of all is that when the anthropologists were asked to reconstruct the likeness of Kino from his skeletal remains, they shrugged and pointed to a sketch on the wall of the City Hall. There hung the drawing done by Mrs. Frances O'Brien of Tucson. One could hardly come any closer to the human reality. She had sketched his portrait from the salient features of the Chini family as they lived in this century. She had only hoped to approximate Kino's likeness. Little did she know she had drawn the last clue in the recognition of Padre Eusebio Kino.

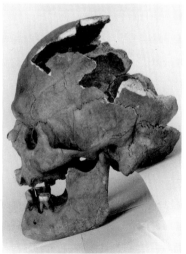

Kino's skull, 1966

THE PADRE KINO MEMORIAL PLAZA

The discovery of Padre Kino's grave in 1966 only set the stage for change in Magdalena. Hardly had the discovery team completed its work before Professor Wigberto Jiménez Moreno suggested that the town be officially renamed "Magdalena de Kino" in the Mexican fashion of commemorating her heroes. Kino's remains could not be left unprotected from the weather or unguarded from the curious and devout. Jiménez Moreno also urged some suitable memorial be designed.

The tiny population of Magdalena had inherited a whole new set of problems that were going to require cooperative efforts to solve. Scientific technicians from the University of Arizona's Department of Anthropology were invited to treat Kino's bones with special preservatives. The soil underneath was impregnated with plasticizers to stabilize the grave site. Covered by a metal roofed shed, a sealed glass vault encased the remains that were left *in situ*.

Patiently, the mayor at the time, Gerardo Nava, looked from his office door on the final resting place of Kino. Streams of visitors passed beside the excavations and impeded the efficiency of operations at city hall. What were the city fathers to do with the grave of a prominent hero at their doorstep? Nava smiled and opened negotiations to move all of the city offices three blocks away to the old Palacio Municipal, which was now serving as one of the city's schools.

So it was that Magdalena waited while federal, state and local officials pondered the proper solution. The care of the grave site passed on to the Instituto Nacional de Antropología e Historia, who designated Gabriel Sánchez de la Vega as chief custodian. Meanwhile the architect Vicente Medel visited Magdalena and devised some initial plans for a monument. The Governor of Sonora Lic. Luis Encinas Johnson, appointed a six man committee of Magdalena citizens to oversee the acquisition of property for the planned monument and to direct the demolition of buildings. Magdalena was on the move.

Then a group of prominent Magdalena citizens, who also served on the Comité del Monumento del Padre Kino, appealed to the Mexican federal government for a change in plans in the development of the Kino monument. Acquiescing to their desires, the government referred the project to the new Governor of Sonora, Faustino Félix Serna. He initiated a completely new plan – more comprehensive, more ambitious and more in accord with the local situation. Subsequently, the architect, Francisco Artigas, who distinguished himself in the colonial restoration of Guanajuato, was invited to design the Plaza of Padre Kino in Magdalena.

Artigas' problem consisted in the integration of several architectural features. The grave was not to be touched; the church was to be remodeled; and a site for a museum and library were to be included. His solution focused each element on a sunken octagonal fountain, thus achieving integration with simplicity and balance. The entire fifteen acre plaza was enclosed by portales (arched, beamed walkways) reminiscent of 18th century building design.

While the details of construction were being worked out, the Comité in Magdalena began the difficult task of relocating the many

Church and Crypt during construction, 1970

Portales that surround the plaza in Magdalena

families who lived in the affected area. Homes the inhabitants considered ancestral were to be leveled for the plaza. With an admirable sense of civic pride, and not without sacrifice, these families moved into newer houses provided in other parts of town. Over 7,000 square yards of buildings were removed to prepare for new construction.

Who paid the bill? Everyone seems to ask. The citizens of Magdalena, individually and through civic groups, contributed over one million pesos toward the ten million peso project. The rest of the financing came through matched donations from the federal and state governments. Cooperation was the key to the Plaza's creation.

In January of 1970 the Constructora Federal de Escuelas Públicas (CAFPCE) began work under the direction of the engineer Francisco Fernández. The restoration of the church was given over to the engineer Juan José Lecanda. Using local materials and labor, architect Gustavo Aguilar from Hermosillo pressed completion of the entire complex by December of the same year.

Before the Plaza was begun, the future president of Mexico, Lic.

Luis Echeverría Alvarez, visited Magdalena in December, 1969. Expressing his admiration for the gigantic labors of Padre Kino in advancing civilization in northwestern Mexico, he solemnly promised to return to inaugurate the memorial plaza. He kept his promise on May 2, 1971; a finished plaza and a proud population awaited him. At noon that day the newly elected President of Mexico visited the crypt while peals of applause welled from the "Pimalteños" who knew their President shared the enthusiasm of their heritage.

More than thirty years have passed since that hot afternoon in May, 1966, when an unexpected fragment of Kino's skull tumbled into the trench of weary searchers. From that moment on, custodians have stood at his grave, day and night. After some ten years had lapsed, the archaeologists noticed that the formaldehyde preservative so cautiously applied in 1966 was wearing thin. Like all humans Kino was turning to dust. Nothing could effectively be done in Magdalena to reverse the process of nature, so officials of INAH sliced away the hardened earth under Padre Kino's skeleton and masterfully encased him in a shock-proof shipping crate. Instead of riding hundreds of hard miles by horse, Kino returned to Mexico City by jet! In a few short weeks the painstaking treatment of the bones was finished and Kino returned to his earthly resting place. At least for the foreseeable future he was not going to crumble to dust.

The domed crypt cloaks a sudden surprise for the casual visitor who may utter a quiet word while looking down at the exposed remains. The architects shaped the crypt and dome to make a perfect contained megaphone so that even whispers can be heard all around the crypt – eliminating the need for guides to use microphones! And often when a visitor approaches the crypt from the sunken plaza, he will see Kino's determined face reflected in one of the windows. This was the clever design of Nereo de la Peña, a Mexican muralist from Caborca who painted the Rivera-esque scenes of Kino's life around the inside of the dome. His artistic talents have even migrated back to Segno, the town of Kino's birth, where Peña decorated the plaza and new museum with murals.

Kino's crypt

Magdalena de Kino now guards the mortal remains of the Padre on Horseback. More splendor than Kino ever knew on the desert trails of the Pimería Alta surrounds him in the plaza that bears his name. He was a man who enjoyed good art and good architecture. He was proud of the churches the Indians had built at Dolores, Remedios and Cocóspera. And he thrilled at the sight of hundreds of his friends coming across the deserts to share in celebrations. Normally drowsy and quiet, the plaza in Magdalena for countless decades has filled with pilgrims to the place where he was buried. First a humble chapel next to Campos' church; next, a separate chapel with a small bell tower; then, nothing but a delapidated ruin shaken by earthquake and rubble under a haughty town hall. The protective architecture had vanished, and Kino lay hidden beneath an ornamental orange tree. Yet, the people kept coming to Magdalena, ostensibly to visit "San Francisco."

One can only wonder how Padre Kino feels now, centuries later, when thousands continue to visit this latest monument erected in his honor.

Karsch photo of Silvercruys' statue

THE STATUES OF PADRE KINO

Statues are made of storied men, but seldom are stories written about statues. This, however, is the story of a storied man and several statues that honor him. The man who first considered Kino an apt subject for monumental art was Father Manuel González, then rector of the mission at Oposura. When Kino was conceiving his great expedition to the Colorado in 1700 to prove that California was not an island, Father González wrote him: "If you accomplish this, we must erect to you a costly and famous statue. And if the way is short, there will be two statues." The way to California was not short, but the accomplishments of Kino's career have already merited him many more than two statues.

The state of Arizona decided to honor Father Eusebio Francisco Kino in 1961 when several Arizona legislators introduced a Joint Memorial (N°. 5) asking that the Congress of the United States accept Padre Kino as the subject for the state's second statue in the National Hall of Statuary. Padre Kino had by that time already been recognized as the state's first pioneer, explorer, and cartographer.

The statue proposal and resolution created new problems because the regulations for statues in the National Hall do not permit purely imaginary conceptions of historical persons. Since the only reputed portrait of Kino was burned in the San Francisco fire of 1907, and no other known portrait of Kino existed, the unusual procedure was devised of creating a likeness from photos of family descendants, using salient and recurrent features. A special committee, designated by Governor Paul Fannin, began an intensive search for a portrait artist. To everyone's satisfaction they commissioned the renowned Tucson artist Frances O'Brien to portray Kino as he may have looked.

Once the portrait was submitted and accepted by the special Kino Memorial Statue Committee all the other pertinent facts about Kino and the dress of his times were compiled into a brochure which was distributed to all sculptors who cared to enter the competition arranged by the statue commission.

From a field of twenty-six entries the committee narrowed the competition to two finalists: George Phippen and Madame Suzanne

Silvercruys. Both of the "competition" statues displayed exemplary skill, remaining faithful to O'Brien's composite portrait, but the rendering of Padre Kino by Baroness Silvercruys conveyed more elements of the historical personage. The committee decided in her favor.

The half-size, plasticine model was shipped to Connecticut where Madame Silvercruys maintained her studio. There she began the complex task of fashioning a seven-foot version of Kino for the National Hall of Statuary. But the attraction of the desert and the figure of Kino brought her frequently to a studio in the foothills of the Catalinas where refinements to the features of the full-sized image were crafted. Finally, molten copper from Arizona mines soon flowed into the precision cast, and Father Kino emerged to take his place among the great founders of this nation.

On February 14, 1965, the first statue of Father Kino was unveiled before a crowd of seven hundred dignitaries from all over the nation and the world. The dedication ceremony took place under the Capitol Rotunda on the same spot where the body of President John F. Kennedy, who had signed the bill admitting Father Kino into the National Hall, had lain in state. It had taken two hundred and sixty-five years, but Father Kino was honored in the way Father González had predicted at the turn of the eighteenth century!

Father Ernest Burrus, S.J., from the Jesuit Historical Institute in Rome, summarized the significance of Kino in his dedicatory address:

Frances O'Brien painting EFK

We can feel justified in dedicating this statue not merely to the memory of one man, however great he may be; we dedicate it to all Americans who would share Kino's high ideals, lofty aspirations, and his bold vision of the future to bring together all peoples in true understanding and in an abiding communion of spirit; we dedicate this statue to the citizens, present and future, of Arizona whose pioneer founder he was; we dedicate it to our neighbors of Mexico, especially to those of Sonora who have preserved his memory in such deep affection; we dedicate it to Kino's native land and to the people and region from which he came; we dedicate it to the peoples of the lands of his adoption, whether in Austria, Bavaria, or Spain, where Kino spent so many of his intensely active years; finally we dedicate this statue of Father Eusebio Francisco Kino to all peoples and to all nations of good will and of high ideals.

These final, ringing words of praise, dedicating the statue, were not final at all. The Mexican delegation realized that Father Kino was more than an Arizona pioneer; he was a symbol even centuries later of the friendship between nations and the dreams of future prosperity. In a matter of weeks the President of Mexico, Gustavo Díaz Ordaz, ordered the grave of Father Kino to be located so that a fitting memorial could be erected to this giant of the Americas.

The tale of discovery constitutes one of those marvels of modern history and archaeological science. Even though no portrait of Kino is extant today, the discovery of his remains

Baroness Silvercruys with models

Martinez Sketch, 1966

in Magdalena has enabled scientists, employing techniques of physical anthropology, and artists to reconstruct his likeness with amazing accuracy.

Realizing the importance of Father Kino to the Mexican-American frontier, Governor Luis Encinas Johnson of Sonora commissioned a famed sculptor in Mexico City to depict Kino on horseback. Don Julián Martínez made a careful study of the skeleton of Kino discovered in Magdalena and formed a powerful figure in bronze to match the man who conquered the desert trails. Two statues were cast. The first was erected in Hermosillo, the capital of Sonora. It now stands at the far northern entrance to the city, dominating the panoramic landscape of the San Miguel and Sonora river valley.

The second statue was presented by Governor Encinas to the Governor and people of Arizona. The spectacular bronze statue was dedicated on the lawn of the capital in Phoenix in an impressive all Spanish program.

Now a statue of Father Kino stands in each capital as a symbol of a common heritage from the man whose dedicated life brought civilization and hope to a previously unknown frontier.

The Arizona dedication ceremonies included a unique look both backward and forward in time. By placing a "time capsule" in the base of the statue Arizonans reviewed their land as it was

Detail of Phoenix statue

64

known to Father Kino, as it was known at the time of the dedication, and as they predicted it to be 272 years from then. It was 272 years before the dedication that Father Kino first set foot in Arizona.

With the dedication of the second statue Padre Manuel González's prediction seemed to be fulfilled. But the gentle padre had miscalculated the ardent appreciation of generations of "Pimalteños." Don Julián Martínez privately confessed that the classic equestrian portrayal of Kino he had done at the request of Governor Encinas was done too rapidly. Despite the excellent quality of his research and his masterful creation of Padre Kino, he felt uncomfortable that he had not captured the soulful essence of the Jesuit missionary. He had sculpted the figure of Kino according to anatomical evidence from the grave; but this was not the younger, vigorous Kino whose visions had transformed the northwest.

Having completed an equestrian statue of Pancho Villa at the request of the President of Mexico which was presented to the City of Tucson, Martínez yearned to do another Kino be-

J. Ivancovich inspects
Hermosillo statue

cause he had learned to love the courageous missionary explorer. And the time was right. In 1987 Arizona and Sonora would celebrate the 300th anniversary of Kino's arrival to the Pimería Alta. What better way to celebrate than to craft a new equestrian statue? But how should the new statue depict Padre Kino? And how could sufficient funds be raised? Martínez conferred with three Jesuits – Fathers Manuel Pérez Alonso, Gabriel Gómez-Padilla and Charles Polzer – and Jorge Olvera. Their stimulating meeting resulted in a decision to portray Kino as a younger man, truly an explorer who would ride the harsh, exhausting desert trails, but still a man of stamina and inspiration. Olvera insisted on conducting a thorough search for authentic tack for the horse and accoutrements for

Kino at north entrance to Hermosillo

the garb of the "Padre on Horseback." Martínez was emphatic that the statue capture Kino's spirit, vision and lofty idealism. Polzer then suggested that all these issues might be resolved if Padre Kino were to clutch an abalone shell in his hands as a symbol of the moment when all Kino's aspirations coalesced in his efforts to reach the abandoned peoples of California. In a matter of weeks Martínez created an intriguing maquette of a resilient missionary-explorer on a tired horse.

The eighteen inch model was completed just prior to Pope John Paul II's historic visit to Arizona. Why not present his Holiness a small memento of the first missionary to the Pimería! Craftsmen at the Desert Crucible, a Tucson foundry, cast the maquette in white bronze just in time for church dignitaries to present him with the statue of a deeply spiritual man about whom he knew nothing! So impressed with the figure of Kino, the Pope changed his prepared remarks, which had lauded the lone missionary so familiar to many, Fray Junipero Serra. Now there was new depth and meaning to the history of the church

Maquette presented
to the Pope

in the West; thousands assembled to hear the pontiff were astonished to hear him speak about this exceptional Blackrobe so dear to the Southwest.

The design for the new statue was firmly in place, but where would the money come from to pay for the full size equestrian? Already the small maquette had created such a positive reaction, talk began to circulate about casting two large bronzes. Julián Martínez coyly lied that two would not be much more expensive than one; in truth, his generosity was incalculable.

Subsequently, a group of citizens in Tucson formed a new committee to head a project called "Three Statues for Three Centuries." If two statues would cost only slightly more than one, why not three? This time the sensitive portrayal of Kino on horseback would be cast in bronze for three places – Tucson, Magdalena, and Segno (Italy)!

Funds poured in from the City of Tucson, Pima County and several generous benefactors. But probably the most generous of all was Don Julián himself because he accepted only $25,000 for all three castings! It was as though Kino's historic generosity were being repaid in kind. The first of the three statues arrived in Tucson in May, 1988, and

Kino statue in Tucson

the statue was erected on the newly completed Kino Parkway. The second statue was completed a year later and erected in Magdalena on the toll road to Hermosillo – a decision of Donaldo Colossio, who held Kino in the highest regard. After all, every traveller in the north would see the hero who put Magdalena on the map, and, anyway, the site was close to the family ranch!

Dedication in Segno, 1991

The third statue experienced some alarming delays, but it was completed in 1990. Following masterful negotiations by Father Gomez-Padilla and Martínez, a Mexican freighter was consigned to ship the enormous bronze to Italy. Although little attention was paid to the venture, this was the first time a heroic, equestrian bronze was sculpted in the Americas and shipped to Europe! The freighter landed in Genoa, from which port the Province of Trent hauled it to the tiny town of Segno where the statue was dedicated in a jubilant celebration in June, 1991. Not even Padre

DeGrazia sketch of Kino

González could have ever dreamed of how many world dignitaries would cross the historic path of Padre Kino – for each of whom Kino held a message of hope and peace.

There is every reason to suspect that southwestern artists will not cease to reinterpret the Padre on Horseback in painting and sculpture. The unique talent of Ted de Grazia was already focused on Father Kino in 1960 in an extensive series of paintings prepared for the 250th anniversary of Kino's death. For a unique issue of *Arizona Highways*, Editor Raymond Carlson invited De Grazia to paint an historic set of twenty views of Kino's life in the Sonoran desert. Ted's sense of simplicity and anonimity, characteristically expressed in bold colors, somehow paralleled his appraisal of Padre Kino for whom he held immense esteem. One can well understand why Father Kino is the subject of art because he embodies an authentic western spirit that encompasses virility, vision, and an awesome sense of peace and purpose.

Most artists have concentrated on Kino's missions and not the man. For many decades picturesque San Xavier del Bac has been the subject of countless paintings and artistic photography. Then, in the aftermath of the discovery of Kino's grave interest flourished in the scores of surviving Jesuit missions. One Tucson artist, Ernie Cabat, repeatedly traveled with mission tour groups to capture the spirit of Mexico and the missions in water colors. Probably many others will join the ranks of Cabat and De Grazia. What the viewer will see will be a church in ruin, but the pervading presence of Padre Kino will still prevail.

One unique tribute was paid Padre Kino by the government of Mexico which issued a special stamp commemorating the 300th anniversary of his arrival in the Pimería Alta. Although strenuous efforts were made by Arizona citizens to have the U. S. Postal Service also issue a commemorative stamp, as they have done for many other pioneers, the Advisory Board vehemently denied him the privilege because they considered him unworthy, too Christian, and not sufficiently American. So Kino stands in the Hall of Statuary each day awaiting the moment when some member of Congress will wonder why this honor was never bestowed.

Arizonans and Sonorans have responded to the memory of Padre Kino in almost every way possible. Statues and paintings have been joined with song and symphony – each being composed for some phase in celebrating the continuing inspiration of this selfless missionary. Corridas were written in Sonora recalling his greatness as a vaquero; Spanish sonnets have honored his memory at village festivals. The Colegio de Kino in Hermosilllo presented a full symphony by a Mexican composer!

Nor has Kino been slighted by the media. After years of work and quiet promotion, Ken Kennedy of Phoenix, Arizona, produced *The Father Kino Story*, first as a two-hour film and later in a one-hour video. *Paths in the Wilderness* appeared as half-hour documentary, placing Kino in the context of the Sonoran desert..

Almost without question artists, authors, and producers will discover Padre Kino again and again because he was a man of the people at a time when the courage and vision of a single man could change the world for the better. He left his home in Europe to find a newer one in the Americas. And as we look back in coming to know him, we find ourselves looking forward in our own times to a future yet to be revealed, equally filled with promise and prosperity. Kino, like the desert he loved, presents us with a paradox of life itself. His legacy is more than history or art; his legacy is faith in the transforming grace of God.

A READING GUIDE FOR MISSION HISTORY

BANNON, JOHN FRANCIS, S.J. *The Spanish Borderlands Frontier, 1513-1821.* New York: Holt, Rinehart and Winston, 1970; 308 pp. One of the better studies on northern New Spain.

BOLTON, HERBERT E. *Padre on Horseback.* San Francisco: Sonora Press, 1932. Reprint, Chicago: Loyola University Press, 1963; introduction by John F. Bannon, S.J.
The Rim of Christendom. New York: Macmillan, 1936. Reprint, New York: Russell and Russell, 1960. Reprint, Tucson: University of Arizona Press, 1984. This remains the definitive biography of Eusebio Francisco Kino.

BURRUS, ERNEST J., S.J. *Kino and Manje, Explorers of Sonora and Arizona.* Rome and St. Louis: Jesuit Historical Institute, 1971. Critical text edition of the Manje diaries.
Kino and the Cartography of Northwestern New Spain. Tucson: Arizona Pioneer's Historical Society, 1965. A complete compilation of known maps by Kino.

CALARCO, DOMENICO. *L'Apostolo dei Pima: Il metodo di evangelizzazione di Eusebio Francesco Chini missionario gesuita pioniere delle Coste del Pacifico (1645-1711).* Bologna: Editrice Missionaria Italiana, 1995. A theological appraisal of Kino's mission methods.

CAVINI, VITTORIO. *L'Avventura di Kino.* Bologna: Editrice Missionaria Italiana della Coop. Sermis, 1990. Kino continues to capture the Italian mind and heart.

DONOHUE, JOHN AUGUSTINE, S. J. *After Kino: Jesuit Missions in Northwestern New Spain, 1711-1767.* Rome and St. Louis: Jesuit Historical Institute, 1969. Mostly about the Pimería Alta up to the expulsion.

ECKHART, GEORGE B. and James S. Griffith. *Temples in the Wilderness: Spanish Churches of Northern Sonora.* Tucson: Arizona Historical Society, Historical Monograph #3, 1975. Brief histories and descriptions of the major churches in the mission chain.

KENNEDY, ROGER. *Mission: The History and Architecture of the Missions of North America.* Edited by David Larkin. Boston: Houghton Mifflin. 1993. Beautiful and informative photographs with a text that presents the strength of the presence of Spanish missions in the United States.

KESSELL, JOHN L. *Mission of Sorrows: Jesuit Guevavi and the Pimas.* Tucson: The University of Arizona Press, 1970. The Pimería Alta missions as seen from the perspective of Guevavi's history.
Friars, Soldiers and Reformers: Hispanic Arizona and the Sonoran Mission Frontier, 1767-1858. Tucson: The University of Arizona Press, 1976. The Franciscan Pimería Alta as seen from the vantage point of Tumacácori mission.

KINO, EUSEBIO FRANCISCO, S. J. *Historical Memoir of the Pimería Alta.* Herbert Bolton, trans. Cleveland: Arthur Clark Co., 1919. 2 vols. Reprint: Berkeley: University of California, 1948. 2 vols. in one.
Kino's Biography of Francisco Javier Saeta. Translated and with an Epilogue by Charles W. Polzer, S. J.; original Spanish transcription edited by Ernest J. Burrus, S. J. Rome and St. Louis: Jesuit Historical Institute, 1971.
Kino's Plan for Development of the Pimería Alta. Ernest J. Burrus, S. J., trans. Tucson: Arizona Pioneer's Historical Society, 1961.
Kino Reports to Headquarters. Ernest Burrus, S. J., trans. Rome: Institutum Historicum Societatis Jesu, 1954.
Kino Writes to the Duchess. Ernest J. Burrus, S. J. trans. Rome: Institutum Historicum SocietatisJesu, 1965.

LOCKWOOD, FRANK C. *With Padre Kino on the Trail*. Tucson: The University of Arizona, 1934. Social Science Bulletin No.5. A scholar/colleague of Bolton with his own view of Kino and the missions.

MANJE, JUAN MATEO. *Luz de Tierra Incognita: Unknown Arizona and Sonora, 1693-1701*. Translated by Harry J. Karns. Tucson: Arizona Silhouettes, 1954. The diaries of Kino's trail companion.

NENTWIG, JUAN. *Rudo Ensayo: A Description of Sonora and Arizona in 1764*. Tucson: The University of Arizona Press, 1980. Translated by Albert F. Pradeau and Robert R. Rasmussen. A good historical overview; caution is urged in the botanical section.

PFEFFERKORN, IGNAZ. *Sonora: A Description of the Province*. Translated by Theodore E. Treutlein. Albuquerque: University of New Mexico Press, 1949. A classic contemporary account.

POLZER, CHARLES W., S. J. *Rules and Precepts of the Jesuit Missions of Northwestern New Spain*. Tucson: The University of Arizona Press, 1976.

PROVINCIA AUTONOMA DI TRENTO. *Padre Kino: L'avventura di Eusebio Francesco Chini, S.J (1645-1711)*. Trento: Provincia di Trento, 1988. Essays on Kino in English, Italian, and Spanish from 1986 Conference.

ROCA, PAUL M. *Paths of the Padres Through Sonora*. Tucson: Arizona Historical Society, 1967. A travelog history of most Sonoran mission sites; historical accounts require critical appraisal.

SMITH, FAY JACKSON, John Kessell, and Francis Fox, S.J. *Father Kino in Arizona*. Phoenix: Arizona Historical Foundation, 1966. This book contains a more complete bibliography on Kino.

SPICER, EDWARD H *Cycles of Conquest: The Impact of Spain, Mexico and the United States on the Indians of the Southwest, 1533-1960*. Tucson: The University of Arizona Press, 1962. The classic anthropological study of the region.

WYLLYS, RUFUS KAY. *Pioneer Padre: the Life and Times of Eusebio Francesco Kino*. Dallas: Southwest Press, 1935. Not as definitive as Bolton's *Rim*, but a deserving life of Padre Kino.

WEBER, DAVID J. *The Spanish Frontier in North America*. New Haven: Yale University Press, 1992. Good background to understand the mission program; generally fair and balanced.

WOODWARD, ARTHUR, and SCOFIELD DELONG and LEFFLER MILLER. *The Missions of Northern Sonora: A 1935 Field Documentation*. Edited by Buford Pickens. Tucson: University of Arizona Press, 1993. Well illustrated and good drawings.

PHOTO CREDITS

All photographs in the book were taken by the author unless otherwise noted in the caption or here below.

Pages 14-25. George Eckhart Collection, Courtesy Arizona State Museum.
Page 26. Photo by Helga Teiwes, Tucson.
Pages 32-41. Courtesy Arizona State Museum.
Page 52. Photo by Edward Ronstadt.
Page 53. Courtesy Instituto de Antropologia y Historia, Mexico.
Page 60. Photo by Yosef Karsch, Ottowa. Courtesy Arizona Historical Society.
Page 64. Sketch by Julián Martínez.
Page 69. Courtesy DeGrazia Foundation.
Back Cover. Photo of DeGrazia painting by Helga Teiwes, Tucson.